AF413633

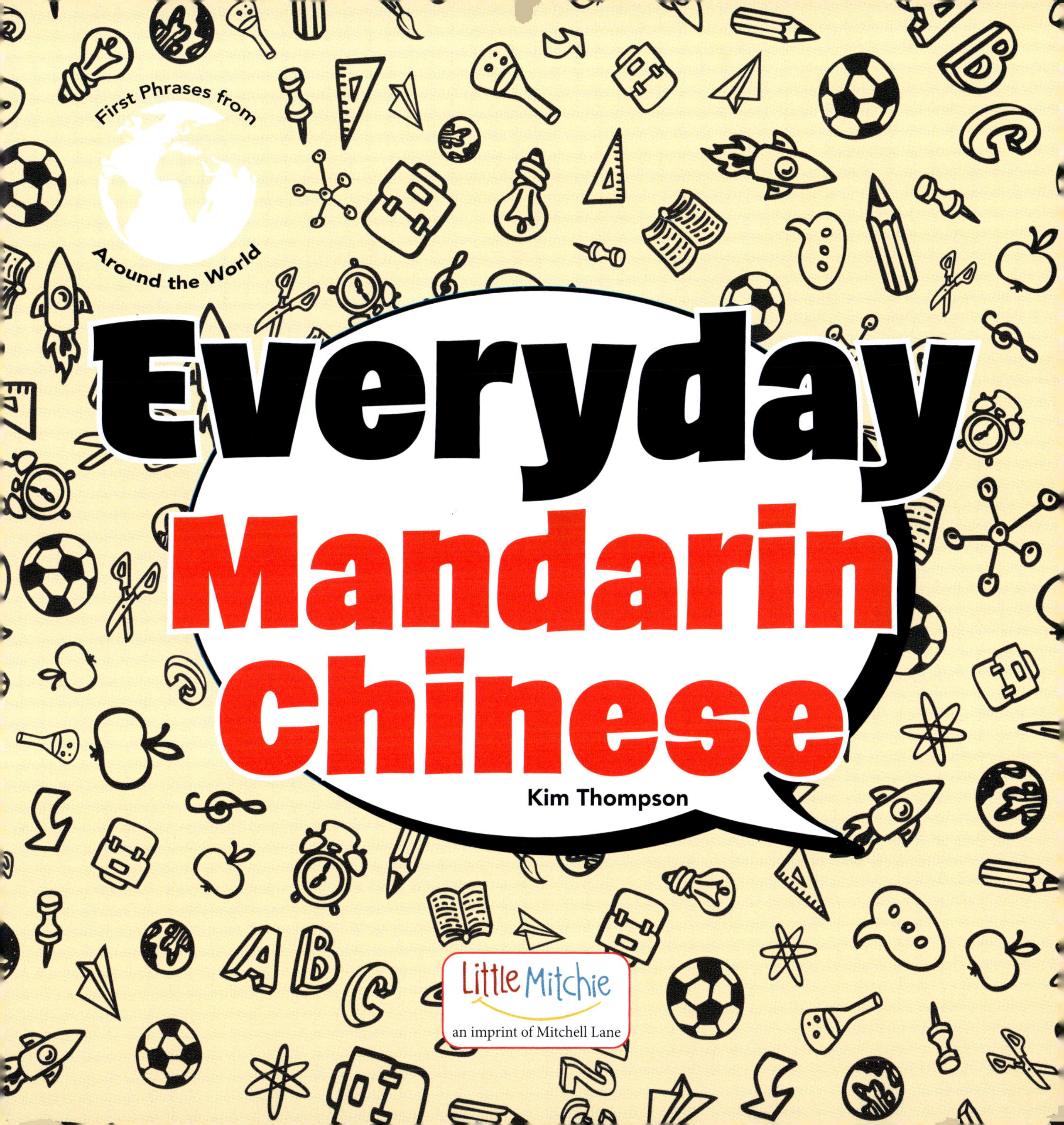
First Phrases from
Around the World
Everyday
Mandarin
Chinese
Kim Thompson
Little Mitchie
an imprint of Mitchell Lane

Creating Young Nonfiction Readers

Little Mitchie lets children delve into nonfiction at beginning reading levels. Young readers are introduced to new concepts, facts, ideas, and vocabulary.

Tips for Reading Nonfiction with Young Readers

Talk about Nonfiction

Begin by explaining that nonfiction books give us information that is true. The book will be organized around a specific topic or idea, and we may learn new facts through reading.

Look at the Parts

Most nonfiction books have helpful features. Our *Little Mitchie* titles include color photographs and graphic aids, a table of contents, and an index. Share the purpose of these features with your reader.

Color Photos and Graphic Aids

A lot of information can be found by "reading" photos, charts, maps, and other graphic aids found within nonfiction texts. Help your reader learn more about the different ways information can be displayed.

Table of Contents

Located at the front of the book, this list shows the big ideas within the text and the page numbers where they can be found.

Index

Located at the back of the book, an index is an alphabetical list of topics and the page numbers where they can be found.

With a little help and guidance about reading nonfiction, you can feel good about introducing a young reader to the world of *Little Mitchie* nonfiction books.

2001 SW 31st Avenue
Hallandale, FL 33009
www.mitchelllanepub.com

First Edition, 2026.

Author: Kim Thompson
Designer: Kathy Walsh
Editor: Tricia Hoffman

Names/credits: Kim Thompson
Title: First Phrases from Around the World
 Everyday Mandarin Chinese
Description: Hallandale, FL:
Mitchell Lane Publishers, [2026]

Series: First Phrases from Around the World
Library bound ISBN: 979-8-89260-542-7
Paperback ISBN: 979-8-89260-584-7
eBook ISBN: 979-8-89260-547-2

Little Mitchie is an imprint of
Mitchell Lane Publishers

PHOTO CREDITS
Cover and Title pg: Adobe Stock: iukhym_vova, smile3377; Doodle Art Adobe: devitaayu, FourLeafLover, wanchana, veekicl, Rizky, mhatzapa, Kebon doodle, Asyam Design, piixypeach, syoko:istock: background, rica nohara; p5, rizal999; p10, Bogdan Malizkiy, jaroon; p 12 Image Source; p13, Bet_noire, EyeEmMobile GmbH; p14, real444, EyeEm Mobile GmbH, gpointstudio; p15, Pongtep Chithan; p16, justocker, EyeEm Mobile GmbH, kool99; p17, real444; p18, M_a_y_a, BongkarnThanyakij, paulaphoto; p20, monkeybusinessimages, kool99, Sorapop, DragonImages; p21, yipengge, zhikun sun, Roxiller, Thai Liang Lim, Vesa Niskanen, Image Source Shutterstock: p4, TimeImage Production, imtmphoto, Ronnachai Palas; p6, Prostock-studio, imtmphoto, Prostock-Studio; p7, Eric Isselee, Aaaarianne; p9, GOLFX; p10, szefei; p 11, GOLFX; p 12, Chiociolla, Chase D'animulls, DongoStock; p15, maroke; p19, PR Image Factory; p22, Hung Chung Chih, Kitreel, New Africa; p23, kwanchai.c

Table of Contents

This Is Me (Zhè jiùshì wǒ) 4

People and Pets (Rén hé chǒngwù) 6

Today (Jīntiān) 8

Morning (Zǎoshang) 10

Breakfast (Zǎocān) 12

School (Xuéxiào) 14

Time to Play (Yóuwán shíjiān) 16

Neighborhood (Línlǐ) 18

Dinner (Wǎncān) 20

Night (Wǎn) 22

Index 24

About Mandarin Chinese 24

This Is Me

Nǐ hǎo!
Hello!
Wǒ bā suìle.
I am eight years old.
Wǒ jiàochūn.
My name is Chun.
4

Zhè jiùshì wǒ

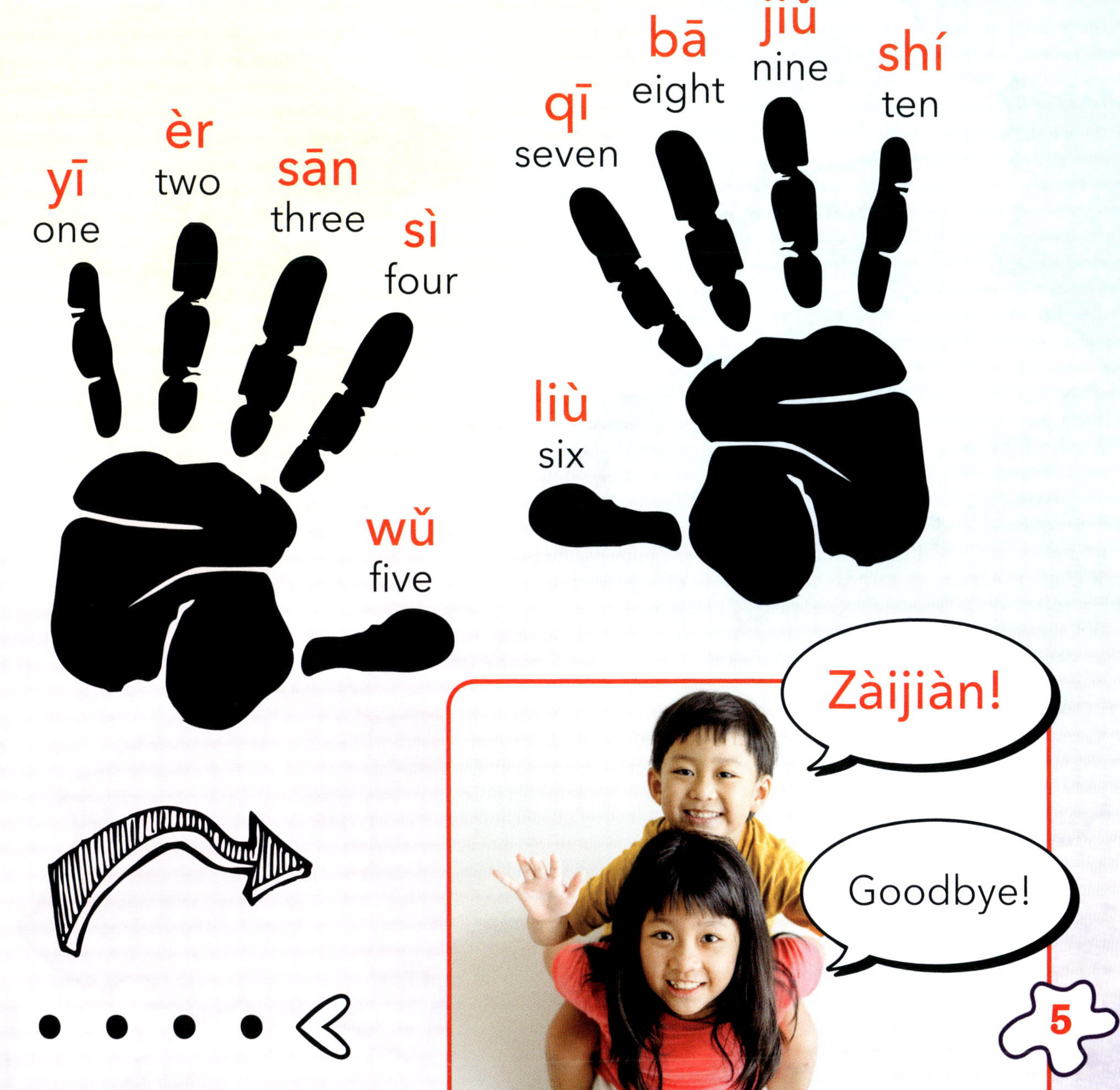

5

People and Pets

fùqīn
father

mǔqīn
mother

gēgē
brother

mèimei
sister

Rén hé chŏngwù

Today

Jīntiān shì xīng qī liù.

Today is Saturday.

xīng qī rì
Sunday

xīng qí yī
Monday

xīng qī èr
Tuesday

xīng qī sān
Wednesday

xīng qī sì
Thursday

xīng qī wǔ
Friday

xīng qī liù
Saturday

Xiànzài yuèfèn shì qī yuè.

The month is July.

yī yuè	January
èr yuè	February
sān yuè	March
sì yuè	April
wǔ yuè	May
liù yuè	June
qī yuè	July
bā yuè	August
jiǔ yuè	September
shí yuè	October
shí yī yuè	November
shí'èr yuè	December

Jīntiān

Wàimiàn hěn rè.
It is hot outside.

yángguāng
míngmèi
sunny

hánlěng
cold

yǔ
rainy

yǒu fēng
windy

9

Morning

Wǒ shūlǐ tóufǎ.
I comb my hair.

Wǒ shuāyá.
I brush my teeth.

Zǎoshang

Wǒ chuān báisè de xié.

I wear white shoes.

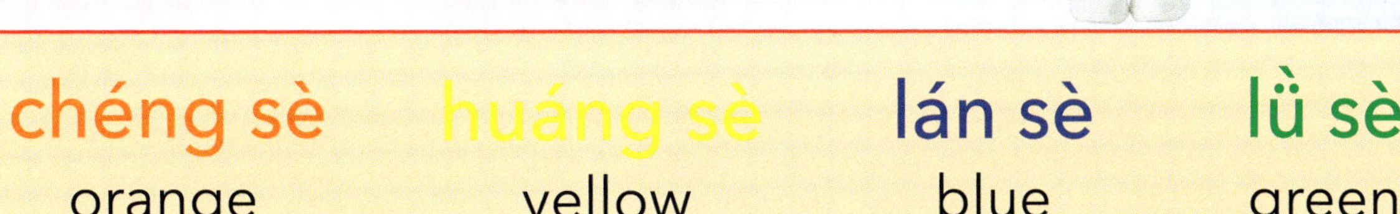

chéng sè	huáng sè	lán sè	lǜ sè
orange	yellow	blue	green

hóng sè	fěn sè	zǐ sè	hēi sè	bái sè
red	pink	purple	black	white

Breakfast

tǔ sī
toast

chéngzhī
orange juice

xūn ròu
bacon

dàn
egg

zǎocān

xiàochē
school bus

bèibāo
backpack

School

Wǒ dú.

I read.

Wǒ zuò shùxué.

I do math.

Xuéxiào

lǎoshī
teacher
shūzhuō
desk

Wǒ xūyào bāngzhù.
I need help.

Wǒ kěyǐ qù xǐshǒujiān ma?
May I go to the bathroom?

Time to Play

Nǐ huì hé wǒ yīqǐ wán ma?
Will you play with me?
Shì de!
Yes!
Wǒ pǎo.
I run.
Wǒ dàng qiūqiān.
I swing.
16

Yóuwán shíjiān

Neighborhood

Wǒ xiàng wǒ de péngyǒu huīshǒu.
I wave to my friend.

Wǒ qù shāngdiàn.
I go to the store.

Línli

Zhège yào duōshǎo qián?
How much does this cost?
dàshà
building
shù
tree
shuǐ
water
huāduǒ
flowers
dānchē
bicycle
rénxíngdào
sidewalk

Dinner

Shì de, qǐng.
Yes, please.

Bùyòngle, xièxiè.
No, thank you.

Dǎrǎo yīxià.
Excuse me.

Wăncān

jiǎozǐ	miàntiáo	fàntuán	yuèbǐng
dumplings	noodles	rice balls	moon cake

hànbǎobāo
hamburger

zhà shǔ tiáo
french fries

Night

Wǒ qù shuìjiàole.
I go to bed.

Wǒ bì shàng
yǎnjīng.
I close my eyes.

Wǎn

zhěntou
pillow

wánjù xióng
teddy bear

23

Index

animals 7

body parts 17

colors 11

days of the week 8

family members 6

foods 12, 21

months of the year 8

numbers 4, 5

shopping 18, 19

weather 9

About Mandarin Chinese

More than one billion people speak Mandarin as their first language. It is the second-most commonly used language in the world after English. Mandarin is widely spoken in Asia and around the world. It is related to other Chinese dialects such as Cantonese and Shanghainese. Mandarin is not based on an alphabet. To write it, you use a separate symbol, or character, to represent each syllable of the spoken language. Mandarin is a tonal language. Using a higher or lower pitch helps to tell one word apart from another.